THIS PICTURE PEARLFECT BOOK BELONGS TO...

_____

BABY, YOU ARE EVERYTHING

WRITTEN AND ILLUSTRATED BY DIAMIN NICOLE

BABY, YOU ARE EVERYTHING

COPYRIGHT© 2020 BY DIAMIN NICOLE
WRITTEN BY DIAMIN NICOLE
PUBLISHED BY IT'S PICTURE PEARLFECT LLC

HARDCOVER ISBN 978-1-7355786-0-6
PAPERBACK ISBN 978-1-7355786-1-3

DEDICATED TO MY
BRAVE, BOLD, AND BEAUTIFUL
DAUGHTER ZARIAH.
ALWAYS SHINE YOUR BRIGHTEST
BABY GIRL.
LOVE ALWAYS, MAMA

LET'S EXPLORE YOUR
IMAGINATION AS YOUR CREATIVITY
REACHES NEW HEIGHTS.

"WATCH OUT! SUPERMAN TO THE
RESCUE, YOU'RE ABOUT TO
SAVE THE NIGHT!"

TELL ME ALL
YOUR SECRETS
I'LL NEVER
TELL A SOUL.
BUILDING TRUST
WITH YOU,
IS SUCH AN
IMPORTANT GOAL.

I'LL ALWAYS BE HERE FOR YOU THROUGH THE LAUGHS, CRIES, AND SHOUTS!

THERE ARE MANY MANY DAYS
WHEN I'M STRESSED TO THE MAX...

BUT YOUR SILLY LITTLE FACES
REMIND ME IT'S OKAY TO RELAX.

SEEING YOU REACH MILESTONES
BRINGS ME OH SO MUCH PRIDE.

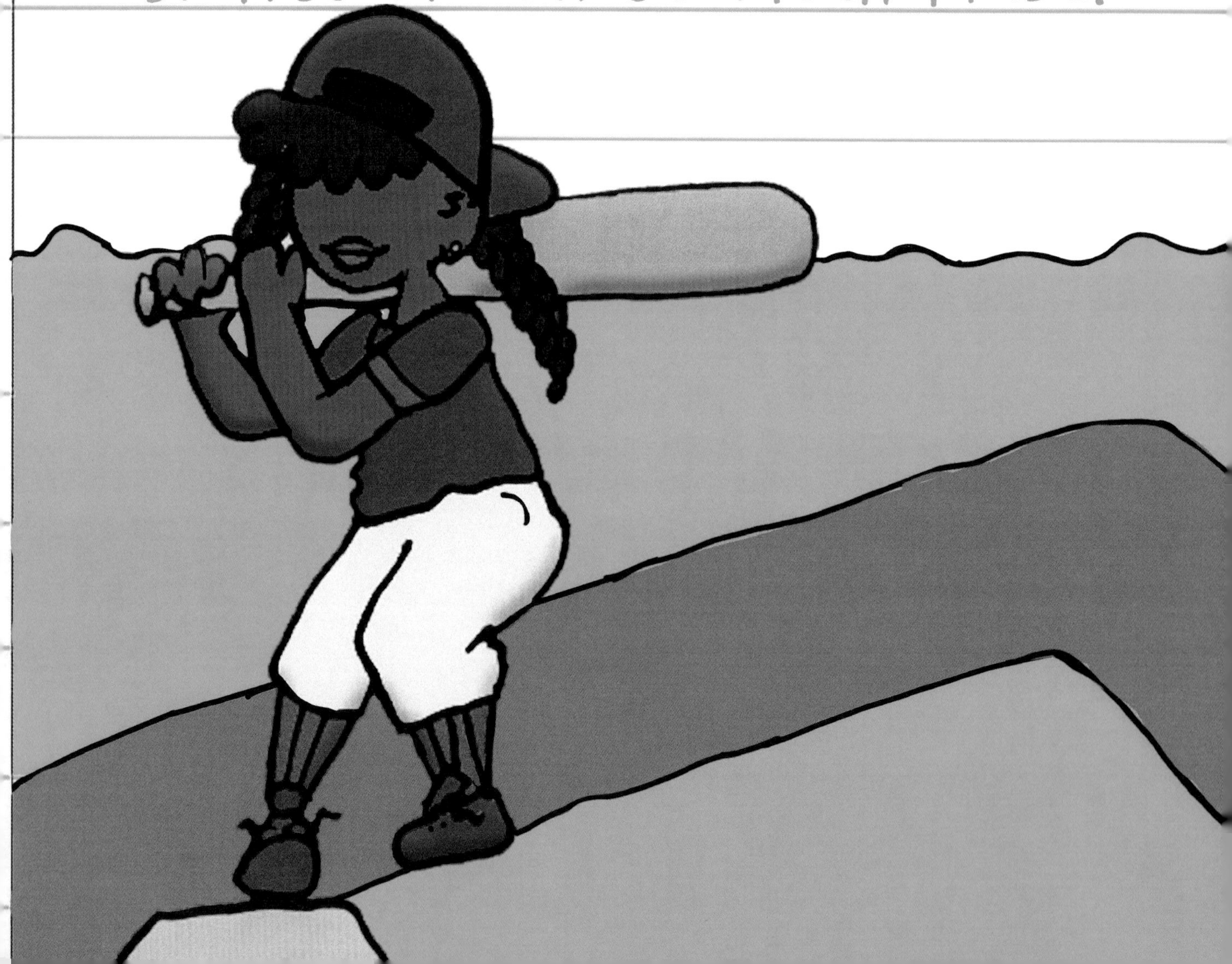

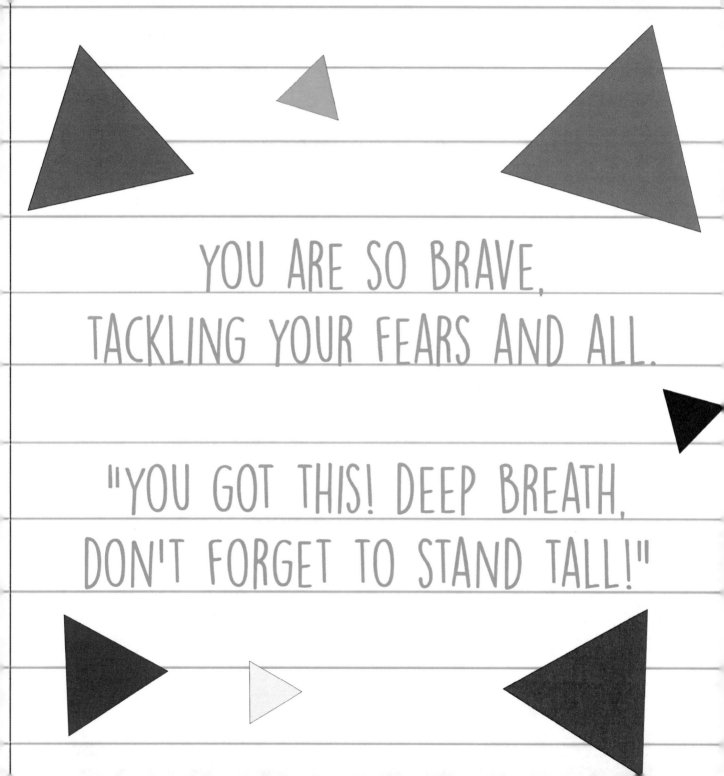

YOU ARE SO BRAVE,
TACKLING YOUR FEARS AND ALL.

"YOU GOT THIS! DEEP BREATH,
DON'T FORGET TO STAND TALL!"

I AM LOVED.
I AM A GIFT.
I AM VALUED.
I AM SPECIAL.
I AM IMPORTANT.
I AM INSPIRING.
I AM ENOUGH.
I AM BEAUTIFUL.

I AM BRAVE.

I AM SMART.

I AM CONFIDENT.

I HAVE A VOICE.

I AM POWERFUL.

I WILL ALWAYS BELIEVE IN MYSELF.

I PROMISE TO MAKE A DIFFERENCE.

BECAUSE I KNOW I AM EVERYTHING!

THAT'S RIGHT BABY, YOU ARE EVERYTHING! I WANT YOU TO DREAM BIG AND YOU DREAM FAR!

YOU INSPIRE ME TO BE BETTER TEACH ME MORE MY LITTLE STAR.

Made in United States
North Haven, CT
12 July 2024

54719819R00015